T0364076

Sugar Skull
ORIGAMI

RUNNING PRESS

PHILADELPHIA

A Running Press® Miniature Edition™

Copyright © 2018 by Running Press

Running Press
Hachette Book Group
1290 Avenue of the Americas, New York, NY 10104
www.runningpress.com
@Running_Press

First Edition: April 2018

Published by Running Press, an imprint of Perseus Books, LLC, a subsidiary of Hachette Book Group, Inc. The Running Press name and logo is a trademark of the Hachette Book Group.

The publisher is not responsible for websites (or their content) that are not owned by the publisher.

ISBN: 978-0-7624-6372-5

9 8 7 6 5 4 3 2

Digit on the right indicates the number of this printing

Contents

Terms to Know

Crease: ———
A line you can see from
a fold that has been made.

Crimp Fold:
Two reverse folds made at
once.

Inside Reverse Fold:
When you make the same
fold in both directions
(mountain and valley).

Mountain Fold: ----------
Backward folds that are
simply valley folds but on the
back of the paper.

Pleat: A fold made by
doubling the paper back
on itself (like a fan).

Squash Fold: A flap in
the paper is squashed flat.

Valley Fold: --------
Forward folds.

Origami

Sugar Skull

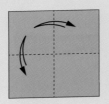

① Colored side up.

② Fold and unfold paper in half along both edges.

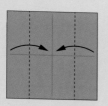

Fold each edge in to the center.

Fold and unfold top right and left corners in.

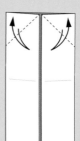

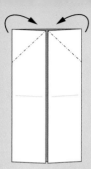

⑤ Inside reverse fold top two corners.

⑥ Fold both flaps down.

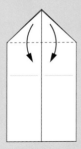

Fold both corners up.

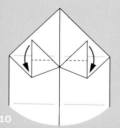

Fold corners back down, making right angle.

10

Fold angle bisectors as shown.

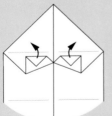

Pull out trapped layers.

Fold flaps outside.

Eyes are finished.

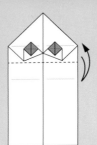

13

Fold and
unfold on dotted
line.

14

Fold out
flaps, creasing
only where
shown.

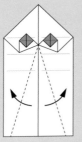

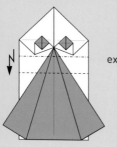

15

Crimp along
existing creases.

16

Fold back flaps
folded out in
Step 14, leaving
paper trapped by
the crimp.

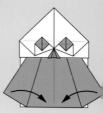

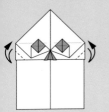

Fold and
unfold.

Inside
reverse fold.

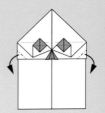

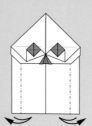

19

Fold and unfold both edges as far as they will go.

20

Fold and unfold lower corners.

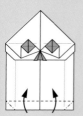

21

Pull up lower edge of paper, squash folding creases made in Step 20.

22

Mountain fold lower section behind.

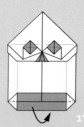

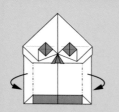

Fold edges behind.

Fold jaw upward.

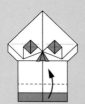

25

Fold over points to round out skull.

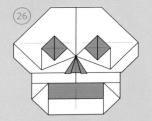

26

Finished.

Top Hat

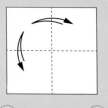

① White side up.

② Fold and unfold paper in half along both edges.

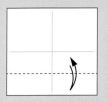

Fold and unfold bottom edge in to the center.

Fold both sides in to the center.

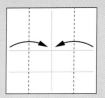

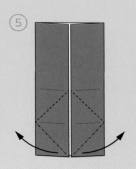

Pull lower two corners
out to sides, folding along crease
made in Step 3.

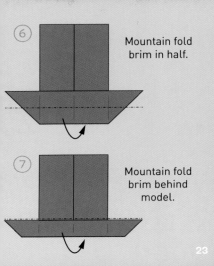

⑥ Mountain fold brim in half.

⑦ Mountain fold brim behind model.

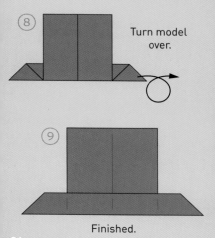

⑧ Turn model over.

⑨ Finished.

Bow Tie

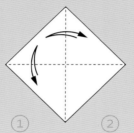

① White side up.

② Fold and unfold along both diagonals.

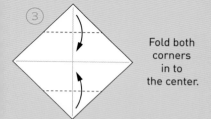

(3)

Fold both
corners
in to
the center.

Fold
two sides
in to
the
center.

(4)

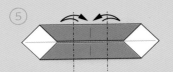

Make two mountain folds
halfway between marked points.

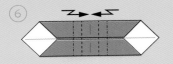

Make two crimps.

⑦ Fold down two corners, stretching and flattening the paper between them.

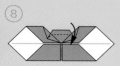

⑧ In progress.

⑨ The result. Repeat on other side.

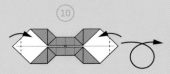

(10)

Fold points of bow tie in
and turn model over.

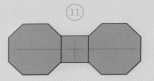

(11)

Finished.

Flower

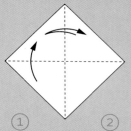

① White side up.

② Fold along both diagonals, leaving one and unfolding the other.

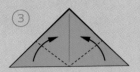

③

Fold both corners
not quite to center line.

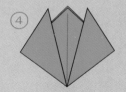

④

Finished.

Leaves

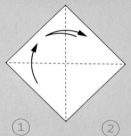

① White side up.

② Fold along both diagonals, leaving one and unfolding the other.

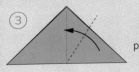

③ Fold one corner past center line.

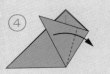

④ Fold corner back, leaving a small crimp.

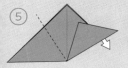

⑤ Pull out the paper trapped in the crimp.

33

Repeat Steps 3–5 on the other side.

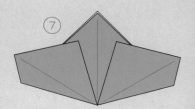

Finished.

Assembly

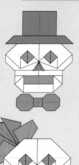

Sugar Skull Man:
Insert head of sugar skull into pocket in top hat. Place bow tie underneath sugar skull.

Sugar Skull Woman:
Insert flower between layers in leaves. Place flower behind sugar skull head.

Before you pick your kirigami design you'll need to create the sugar skull base. Before making any cuts, use a pencil to mark the pattern on the paper to help guide your cuts (use a ruler). You might also consider making a larger copy of the templates to fit the size of your paper.

Kirigami

Sugar Skull Base

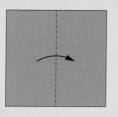

① Colored side up.

② Fold in half from one edge to opposite edge.

Make a pinch halfway
down folded edge.

Using this diagram
as a guideline, use a
pencil to mark the sugar
skull outline on your
paper and cut
out the skull shape.

Using the
pinch from Step 2
as a reference,
cut out nose.

Fold slightly
past halfway point;
line up
with jaw.

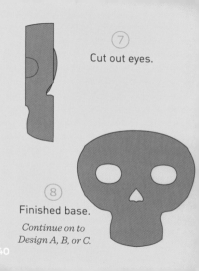

⑦ Cut out eyes.

⑧ Finished base.

Continue on to Design A, B, or C.

Skull base template

Design A

① Start from sugar skull base (p. 37) and use Design A template for reference (p. 45).

② Cut out eyebrows and eye markings, then unfold.

Cut out
forehead marking
and nose
detail.

Fold mouth area
in half.

Cut out lip and
mouth detail and
unfold all.

6 Finished.

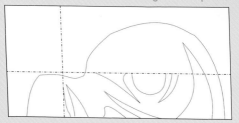

Design B

1. Start from sugar skull base (p. 37) and use Design B template for reference (p. 49).

2. Cut out eyebrows and eye markings, then unfold.

Cut out forehead
markings.

Fold mouth area
in half.

5

Cut out lips
and teeth and
unfold all.

6

Finished.

Design B template

Design C

① Start from sugar skull base (p. 37) and use Design C template for reference (p. 54).

② Cut out eyebrows and eye markings, then unfold.

Fold in half.

Cut out additional markings, then unfold.

5

Cut out forehead
markings,
nose detail, and
chin detail.

6

Fold a pleat at a
slight angle. The outer
mountain folds should
be the same
distance from the
center. valley fold.

⑦ Cut out teeth and unfold all.

⑥ Finished.

Design C template

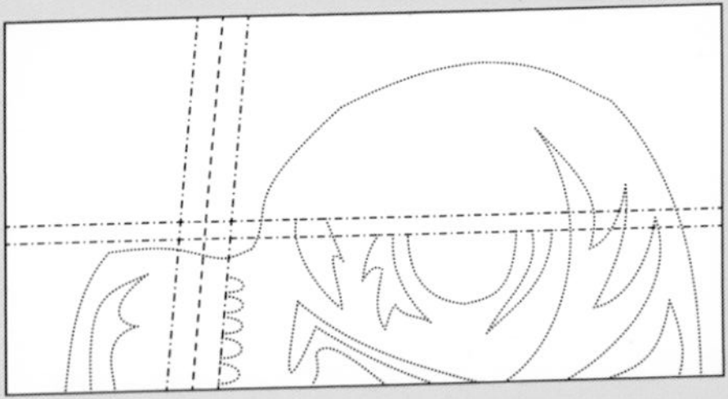

This book has been
bound using handcraft methods
and Smyth-sewn
to ensure durability.

Written by
Peter Marchetti.

Designed by Jason Kayser.